Studying Through I Samuel

44 Daily Bible Studies for Understanding & Application

<u>Joshua 1:8</u>: This book of the law shall not depart out of thy mouth; but thou shalt meditate therein day and night, that thou mayest observe to do according to all that is written therein: for then thou shalt make thy way prosperous, and then thou shalt have good success.

James Bussard

All Scripture quotations are from the *Authorized (King James) Version of the Bible.*

Any definitions or commentaries came from the following three sources:

1. Strong's Exhaustive Concordance of the Bible

2. Thayer's Greek Lexicon

3. Webster's 1828 Dictionary

Any definitions and commentaries provided are given as accurately as possible, and are based upon the sources listed above. These studies do in no way proclaim themselves to be without error, even though the utmost care was taken to be accurate and faithful to the Word of God.

These studies were developed for a person using the *Authorized (King James) Version of the Bible.* A person that uses these studies with other versions may not be able to use them as efficiently.

<u>Preface</u>

They say that necessity is the mother of invention. This book came about out of necessity. My wife teaches a group of teenage girls, at our church, and found out that they did not know how to study or apply the Bible. Thus, they were reading it, but getting little from their reading, with no knowledge of how to apply it.

I had already done a series of studies on the book of John that were a bit more in-depth, but light on application. So, this book came about to fulfil several purposes:

1.) To provide a short, but interactive, source of daily devotional material for application

2.) To point out certain specific applications from each passage

3.) To emphasize the stories of the Bible, and the doctrine that lies therein

This book is not written to provide my opinions on Scripture (though some of that will, no doubt, leak through), but to teach the reader how to appreciate context, think objectively, interpret properly, and apply successfully. When these things happen, the believer in Jesus Christ grows in the faith.

These studies have already helped our Youth Group, because they are learning to read, interpret, and apply the Bible to their lives. They are growing in the Lord, and you will too.

Let me be clear: you will not grow, because I am a great writer, pastor, or whatever. You will grow, because God has promised that we will, if we observe to do what is written in His Word (***Romans 10:17; I Peter 2:2***). It is God alone that gives every believer in Jesus Christ of His Spirit, to understand the scriptures, faith to obey, and ability to grow. He alone gets the glory for anything good that comes of this book.

If I can answer any questions or you have any comments that come about, as you study through this book, please feel free to reach out to me at *PastorBussard@Gmail.com*.

Best Regards,

James Bussard, Pastor
Pinecrest Baptist Church, Signal Mountain, TN

Brief Outline of I Samuel

I. Samuel (1-9) – The Last Judge

    A. Samuel's Birth (1:1-2:36)

    B. Samuel's Ministry (3:1-8:22)

II. Saul (9-15) – The First King

    A. Saul is Chosen (9:1-12:25)

    B. Saul is Rejected (13:1-15:35)

III. David (16-31) – The Man after God's Own Heart

    A. David is Chosen (16:1-23)

    B. David is Called Out (17:1-18:30)

    C. David is Chased (19:1-29:11)

    D. David is Corrected (30:1-31:13)

<u>Read I Samuel 1:1-11: Hannah Prays for a Child</u>

1. What man lived in Mount Ephraim (*v.1*)?____

2. What were the names of his two wives (*v.2*)? ___________________________________

3. Which wife had no children (*v.2*)? ____

4. Where did Elkanah go up yearly to worship (*v.3*)?______________________________

5. What were the names of Eli's two sons (*v.3*)? __________________________________

6. When Elkanah offered, what did he give to Hannah (*v.5*)? _______________________

7. Why (*v.5*)?____

8. What did Hannah's adversary do to her (*v.6*)?

____

9. When this would happen, what would Hannah do (*v.7*)? _________________________

10. Who sat by a post of the temple of the Lord (*v.9*)? ____________________________

11. What was the state of Hannah's soul? (*v.10*)? ________________________________

12. What did Hannah promise to do, if God gave her a son (*v.11*)?

____

13. What did she say would never come upon his head (*v.11*)? _____________________

<u>Applications</u>:

1. God's Word is to be our handbook for daily living. In it, God lays out His plan for mankind. He tells us of our fall into sin, the consequences thereof, and that salvation is available through Jesus Christ. He also tells us of His design for the family. God's design for the Christian home is one man marrying one woman for life. In this passage, we see the strains of going outside of God's design. Elkanah had two wives that were adversaries. Because Peninnah had children, she provoked Hannah, who did not, which caused her to fret terribly. If Elkanah would have chosen to do things God's way, this problem would not have existed. What about you? Are you playing God's mandated role for your life right now? What is that role and how are you playing it well?

____

____

____

2. Hannah vowed a vow to God that she did not break. She promised to give God her child, and did. God's Word warns us to be careful of making such promises. If we decide to promise something to God, then we need to make good on our promise. God takes such things very seriously. Have you ever made a vow to God? What was it? Have you held up your end of the bargain to God?

____

____

____

____

____

____

Write down one or more of the above applications that spoke to you personally, and pray that God will help you with it. If you have questions (or need help with application), please speak with your pastor/teacher:

____

____

____

<u>Read I Samuel 1:12-28: Hannah Prays for a Child (Part Two)</u>

1. What did Eli notice about Hannah (*v.12-13*)?

____

2. Because of this, what did he assume about her (*v.13*)?_____________________

3. Instead of drinking wine or strong drink, what did Hannah say that she had done (*v.15*)?

____

4. After praying and speaking with Eli, what happened to Hannah (*v.18*)?

____

5. In response to her prayer, what did God do for Hannah (*v.20*)?

____

6. What did she call her son (*v.20*)? __________________________________

7. Why (*v.20*)? ____

8. When did Hannah tell Elkanah that she would resume going to the yearly sacrifice (*v.22*)?

____

9. When this happened, who did they bring Samuel to (*v.25*)? ____________________

10. Because God answered her prayer, what did Hannah do with Samuel (*v.28*)?

____

<u>Applications</u>:

1. Hannah was in such emotional distress that she could not even give voice to her prayers. Instead, she could only move her mouth and pray with her heart. Nonetheless, God heard and answered her prayer. Have you ever had a time when you felt that you could not voice your prayers? When was this? Did you pray with your heart? How did God answer that prayer? It is wonderful to know that we have a Father that loves His children so!

____

____

____

____

2. Hannah's faith drove her to pray. Her heart was aggrieved and, instead of curling up in a corner and falling into depression, she went to pray to her God. This woman is a great example of how we ought to act. When troubles come our way, we must pray! When was a time that great troubles came into your life? Did you pray? How did God answer? Will you determine to run to God in prayer, when troubles come your way, in the future?

____

____

____

____

____

3. After Hannah prayed, Eli worked to encourage her. Because of her faith, and the priest's encouragement, she was at peace. Scripture tells us to come to Christ, lay our burdens upon Him, and trust in His ability to take care of us. Jesus only wants us to have one burden in this life: that of following Him. He promises to take care of the rest (*Matt 11:28-30*). Do you believe this? When you have a heavy burden, do you run to God in prayer and leave it with Him, or do you carry your heavy burdens around with you every day? Will you work to trust Christ with your life?

____

____

____

____

____

Write down one or more of the above applications that spoke to you personally, and pray that God will help you with it. If you have questions (or need help with application), please speak with your pastor/teacher:

____

____

____

Read I Samuel 2:1-10: Hannah's Prayer

1. Who did Hannah say that her heart rejoiced in (*v.1*)? _______________________________________

2. Why did she say that her mouth was enlarged over her enemies (*v.1*)?

____

3. Who did Hannah say was as holy as the Lord (*v.2*)?____

4. For what two reasons should we not allow pride and arrogance to come out of our mouths (*v.3*)?

    a. ____

    b. ____

5. What did God do to the bows of the mighty (*v.4*)? ____

6. What did He do for those that stumbled (*v.4*)?

____

7. What did God allow to happen to those that were full (*v.5*)?

____

8. What did He do to the barren (*v.5*)?____

9. What happened to the woman that had many children (*v.5*)?

____

10. Why was God able to kill, make alive, make poor and rich, and raise beggars (*v.8*)?

____

____

11. What is God's promise to His saints (*v.9*)? ____

12. What will happen to the adversaries of the Lord (*v.10*)?

____

<u>**Applications**</u>:

1. Hannah stated that her horn was exalted in the Lord. This is speaking of her reliance upon God's power in her life. The God of the Bible is the Almighty God. He can do anything, and with Him all things are possible. Hannah believed this. Do you? When was a time in your life that God proved His almighty power to you?

____

____

____

____

2. Hannah also spoke about God being her rock. When Scripture speaks of this, in regards to God, it is usually speaking of the foundation of our lives. What is your life founded upon? Is it founded upon the Person, Work, and Teaching of Jesus Christ, or something else? Many people found their lives upon their parents, friends, the media, opinions, experiences, or other things/people. Hannah founded hers upon her God. What about you? What will you found your life upon and follow the rest of your days?

____

____

____

3. Hannah then spoke about God's ability to do whatsoever He pleases. We call this God's Sovereignty. Our God is our Creator and the King of the Universe, thus, He can do whatever He wishes. Hannah spoke about God creating the rich and poor, about Him bringing people down low, and lifting them up. Do you believe that God can do as He wishes in the Universe? What about you personally? Have you yielded your will to God, to accept His plan for your life? In what ways have you already seen God direct your life, according to His will?

____

____

____

Write down one or more of the above applications that spoke to you personally, and pray that God will help you with it. If you have questions (or need help with application), please speak with your pastor/teacher:

____

____

Read I Samuel 2:11-21: The Wickedness of Eli's Sons

1. Who returned to his house in Ramah (*v.11*)?_______________________________________

2. Who did Samuel minister unto the Lord before, at the Tabernacle (*v.11*)?_______________________

3. What type of people were Eli's sons (*v.12*)?_______________________________________

4. What does this phrase mean (*v.12*)? _______________________________________

5. What was the priest's custom, when the flesh of a sacrifice would be seething on the altar (*v.13-14*)?

____

____

6. What did the priest's servant want from the people that sacrificed, instead of sodden flesh (*v.15*)?

____

7. If a person wanted to burn the fat first, how did Eli's sons reply (*v.16*)?

____

____

8. How did God view the sins of the young men (*v.17*)? _______________________________________

9. Why was this so (*v.17*)? _______________________________________

10. Who ministered before the Lord (*v.18*)? _______________________________________

11. What was he girded with (*v.18*)? _______________________________________

12. What would his mother bring him every year (*v.19*)? _______________________________________

13. After Eli blessed Elkanah and Hannah, what did God do for them (*v.21*)?

____

14. What did Samuel continue to do (*v.21*)? _______________________________________

<u>**Applications**</u>:

1. Instead of obeying the Law of God, Eli's sons rejected its rules in favor of their own lusts. In fact, they threatened violence against people that tried to get them to do right! There are those that love the Word of God, and those that do not. Which are you? Do you study the Bible unto obedience and application? What are you working on applying to your life right now?

____

____

____

2. Because Hannah loaned Samuel to the Lord, God blessed her with more children. When we love the Lord, follow Him, and obey His Word, the result is always blessing. Now, we should not expect God's blessing to be in the form of material things. This is a faulty teaching of the world. Instead, we need to understand that His blessing is always poured out of His grace. God's grace could take the form of wisdom, peace, joy, protection, and many other things that we so desperately need in this troubled world. We deserve none of these things, but God is so good to pour His grace upon us. How has God been gracious to you recently? How has He blessed you?

____

____

____

____

____

____

Write down one or more of the above applications that spoke to you personally, and pray that God will help you with it. If you have questions (or need help with application), please speak with your pastor/teacher:

____

____

____

<u>**Read I Samuel 2:22-36: God Rejects Eli**</u>

1. How old was Eli, when he heard of the evil that his sons did (*v.22*)? _______________________

2. When he reproved them for their sinful acts, what was their response (*v.25*)?

____

3. Why was this so (*v.25*)? ____

4. Who did Samuel grow to be in favor with (*v.26*)? __________________________________

5. What did God say that Eli had done with His sacrifice and offering (*v.29*)?

____

6. What did He say that Eli had done with his sons (*v.29*)?

____

7. Why had Eli done this, in God's eyes (*v.29*)?

____

8. What did God promise to do to Eli (*v.32*)?

____

9. What was the sign that God promised to give, to confirm His promise (*v.34*)?

____

10. Who did He promise to raise up (*v.35*)?____

11. What did God promise to do for him (*v.35*)?

____

<u>**Applications**</u>:

1. Eli did not teach his children to love the Lord. Therefore, they were wicked. In the Bible, God tells parents that He gives them children, to train up for His glory (*Deut 6:4-9*). Literally, children are the greatest ministry of their parents. If the parents lose their children to the Devil, then they have failed. Should God give you children one day, will you determine to teach them to follow God and His Word? If you already have children, are you carefully, purposefully raising them to follow Christ?

____

____

2. Because of Eli's lack of parenting, God sent a man to him with a sad message of judgment. He promised to kill Eli's sons and remove the priesthood from his family. All of this happened, because Eli honored his sons above God and His Word. Many parents do the same today. They believe they are showing their children love by giving them whatever they desire and never/rarely punishing them. Instead, such parents are cursing their children to a terrible fate. If you have children, will you determine to discipline them, when they need it, and train them properly? If God should give you children in the future, will you determine to do these things? God tells the parent that disciplines properly that they are delivering their child from Hell (*Prov 23:14*). Just so, we understand that the parent who refuses to correct their child is only working to send them to Hell.

____

____

____

3. We can pull another lesson from Eli's faulty parenting. God told the priest that he honored his children above Him. This means that Eli made his sons to be his idols over God. Many parents fall into the trap of idolizing their children. In doing this, they ignore God and His Word, and cater to the whims of their children. This is a tragic mistake with often eternal consequences. Who do you worship? Do you worship the God of Heaven and seek to obey His Word, or do you worship something/someone else? Whose advice do you value and heed above all others? Who do you love above everyone else? If we are Christians, we must choose to love and follow Christ.

____

____

____

____

Write down one or more of the above applications that spoke to you personally, and pray that God will help you with it. If you have questions (or need help with application), please speak with your pastor/teacher:

____

____

____

<u>Read I Samuel 3:1-12: God Reveals Himself to Samuel</u>

1. Why was the Word of the Lord precious, in those days (*v.1*)?

____

2. What had happened to Eli (*v.2*)?

____

3. Who was laid down to sleep (*v.3*)? ____

4. Who called unto Samuel (*v.4*)? ____

5. What was Samuel's answer (*v.4*)? ____

6. Who did Samuel think was calling him (*v.5*)? ________________________________

7. What did Eli say about the matter (*v.5*)?

____

8. Why did Samuel think that it was Eli calling him (*v.7*)?

____

____

9. What did Eli tell Samuel to say, the next time the Lord called him (*v.9*)?

____

10. What did God say would happen to the ears of everyone that heard about what He would do (*v.11*)?

____

11. What did He say that He would perform against Eli (*v.12*)?

____

<u>**Applications**</u>:

1. The Bible states that Samuel and Eli lived in a day where there was no open vision of the Lord. We could say that we live in a day like that. After God finished the Book of Revelation, the canon of Scripture was closed, and He ceased giving new revelation. Therefore, the Bible ought to be very precious to us, as it alone contains the words that God has given to mankind! How precious is the Bible to you? Do you read it every day? Do you read it for reading or for study? Do you record what God speaks to you about? Do you seek to apply these things to your life? God's Word ought to be extremely precious to every believer.

____

____

____

2. Samuel was left by Hannah to serve the Lord in the Tabernacle. Indeed, he did serve. However, though he served, the young man did not know the Lord personally. In other words, he had no relationship with Him. Through this, we learn an important lesson: service for God does not mean that we know Him. We live in a day where many people think they know the Lord, because they do much in His name. Jesus even states that such will be surprised at the Day of Judgment, when they are rejected by Him, because they never knew Him (***Matt 7:21-27***)! No, service does not equal spirituality. Only spirituality equals spirituality. So, how is a person spiritual? Only by following Christ through faithful reading, study, and application of the Word of God. How about you? How is your relationship with Christ? Do you focus on reading, studying, and applying God's Word, or are you relying on your service to Him, to gain His favor? What is the last thing that God spoke to you about in His Word? How are you working to apply this to your life?

____

____

____

____

Write down one or more of the above applications that spoke to you personally, and pray that God will help you with it. If you have questions (or need help with application), please speak with your pastor/teacher:

____

____

____

<u>**Read I Samuel 3:13-21: God Reveals Himself to Samuel (Part Two)**</u>

1. Why did God promise to judge Eli's house forever (**v.13**)?

____

2. What had Eli's sons done (**v.13**)? _______________________________________

3. What did Eli neglect to do (**v.13**)?_______________________________________

4. How did Samuel feel about showing Eli the vision that God gave him (**v.15**)? ___________________

5. What did Eli want Samuel to tell him (**v.17**)?

____

6. Did Samuel hide anything from Eli (**v.18**)? _______________________________

7. What was Eli's response (**v.18**)?

____

8. As Samuel grew, who was with him (**v.19**)? _______________________________

9. What did God do for Samuel (**v.19**)?

____

10. What did all of Israel know about Samuel (**v.20**)?

____

<u>**Applications**</u>:

1. God determined to judge Eli's house, because he did not restrain his sons from doing evil. It is the parents' job to train their children to live a righteous life. Furthermore, it is their job to discipline the children, when they get out of line. The Bible calls this chastisement. No parent *wants* to chastise their children, but it is *necessary* to teach the difference between right and wrong. If no chastisement is given, then only wickedness comes (like what we see with Eli's children). If you have children, do you correct them, or do you allow them to do whatever they wish? Do you teach them to live a holy life, or do you neglect to teach them at all? How do you teach your children? If you fail in any of these areas, will you determine to do things God's way, for your children's sake? If you do not have children, will you determine to raise them for the Lord, should He give them to you?

____

____

2. Eli demanded the truth from Samuel, who gave it to him (though he was afraid). For all his faults, when Eli heard the declaration of the Lord, he accepted it as God's will. God declares many things in His Word. He tell us His way of salvation through Jesus Christ. He also tells us how to live a righteous life before Him. These things are part of His will for us. Have you surrendered to God's will for your life? What do you know that you need to surrender to and do now, by faith, to please Him? If you have never surrendered to God's will, will you right now?

____

____

____

3. Samuel was a young man that was developing a relationship with the God of Heaven. As such, it was apparent to those around him that he followed God, and was appointed to be a prophet. As believers, our lives are to reflect God's transforming work in our lives. This work becomes more apparent, as we follow Christ by obeying His Word. Have you accepted Jesus Christ as your personal Savior? Do others know about this? How do they know? What changes have others seen in your life, since you have been saved, that prove God's transforming work in your life? What changes have they seen recently?

____

____

____

____

____

____

____

Write down one or more of the above applications that spoke to you personally, and pray that God will help you with it. If you have questions (or need help with application), please speak with your pastor/teacher:

____

____

____

Read I Samuel 4:1-11: Hophni and Phinehas Are Slain

1. Who did Israel go out to battle against (*v.1*)? _______________________________________

2. Who ended up winning that battle (*v.2*)?____

3. About how many people were killed (*v.2*)? ____

4. What did the elders of Israel decide to fetch (*v.3*)? ___________________________________

5. Why (*v.3*)? ____

6. Who were with the Ark of the Covenant (*v.4*)? _______________________________________

7. When the ark came, what did the people do (*v.5*)?

____

8. When the Philistines heard this, how did they feel (*v.7*)? ______________________________

9. What did they say about the situation (*v.7*)?

____

10. What did they have to say about Israel's God (*v.8*)?

____

11. Why did they encourage each other to be strong and like men (*v.9*)?

____

12. Who ended up winning the upcoming battle (*v.10*)?___________________________________

13. How many men of Israel were killed (*v.10*)? ____

14. What happened to the Ark of the Covenant (*v.11*)? ___________________________________

15. Who was also slain (*v.11*)? ____

<u>**Applications**</u>:

1. Israel made a grave error in bringing the Ark out of Shiloh. They assumed that bringing a relic into a battlefield would magically save them: turning the tide in their favor. In fact, their idolatry only made matters worse. God wants us to trust in Him, not relics. He wants us to put our faith in His Word, not our own strength. Do you put your faith in God and God's Word, or do you trust in a relic or image?

____

____

2. God had told Eli that his sons would die in one day, and they did. We do not know how much time passed between the giving of the prophecy and fulfillment, but we know that God always keeps His promises. Do you believe that God keeps His promises? What is one promise that has stood out to you recently, during your Bible reading? What promises has God kept for you recently?

____

____

____

____

Write down one or more of the above applications that spoke to you personally, and pray that God will help you with it. If you have questions (or need help with application), please speak with your pastor/teacher:

____

____

____

<u>**Read I Samuel 4:12-22: The Ark of the Covenant Is Stolen**</u>

1. Who ran to Shiloh (***v.12***)? ____

2. Who was sitting by the wayside watching (***v.13***)? ______________________________

3. Why (***v.13***)? ____

4. When the messenger told the message of the ark's capture, how did the city respond (***v.13***)?

____

5. How old was Eli (***v.15***)? ____

6. What was the state of his eyes (***v.15***)? ______________________________________

7. When the messenger told Eli about the ark being taken, what happened (***v.18***)?

____

8. How long had Eli judged Israel (***v.18***)? _____________________________________

9. When Phineas' wife heard the news, what happened (***v.19***)?

____

10. Did she give birth to a son or daughter (***v.20***)? _____________________________

11. What did Phineas' wife name her child (***v.21***)? ______________________________

12. Why (***v.21***)? ____

<u>**Applications**</u>:

1. Scripture tells us that Eli's heart trembled for the Ark of God. In other words, he had more care for a relic than he did for the very Word of God. Later on, the Ark's theft affected the priest so much that he fell off his chair, broke his neck, and died. What do you put your faith in? Do you trust in God and God's Word, or do you trust in relics and statues? Many religions put their faith in the latter, but True Christians trust in the former. What do you? What Bible passage are you putting your faith in right now? How are you applying it to your life?

____

____

____

____

2. Because of the Ark being stolen, Phinehas' wife gave her son the name Ichabod, which means *the glory has departed*. The Ark of the Covenant was a symbol of God's presence among His people, and its theft represented His presence departing. Sadly, many homes and churches have lost the presence of God's Spirit, because of their refusal to obey His Word. How about you? Is God's presence on your life? What about your home? Your church? Is God present, or is He absent? How do you know these things? Please list your reasons below:

____

____

____

____

____

____

____

Write down one or more of the above applications that spoke to you personally, and pray that God will help you with it. If you have questions (or need help with application), please speak with your pastor/teacher:

____

____

____

<u>Read I Samuel 5:1-12: God Smites the Philistines</u>

1. Where did the Philistines bring the Ark of the Covenant (**v.1**)? _______________________________

2. What place did they bring it into (**v.2**)? ____

3. When they went there the next morning, what did the Philistines find (**v.3**)?

____

4. What did they do with Dagon (**v.3**)? ____

5. The next day, in addition to being fallen, what else had happened to Dagon (**v.4**)?

____

6. What did the Lord do to those of Ashdod (**v.6**)? ____

7. Where did the people of Ashdod bring the ark to (**v.8**)? ___________________________________

8. What did God do to the men of that place (**v.9**)?

____

9. Where did the people of Gath bring the ark to (**v.10**)? ____________________________________

10. Why did the people of that place say that the ark was brought to them (**v.10**)?

____

11. What did the lords of the Philistines determine to do with the ark (**v.11**)?

____

12. Why (**v.11**)? ____

<u>Applications</u>:

1. God smote both the statue of the false god Dagon and the Philistines themselves, to make a point: God is the True God of the Universe, and there is none else. Therefore, the gods of this world are false ones that have no power against the True, Living God. Do you believe this? Is the God that you believe in the True and Living God, or some false, dead one? How strong is your God? Is He able to save you from your sin? Is He able to keep you saved? Is He able to help and keep you, as you live for Him?

____

____

____

2. God's work among the Philistines produced the intended result: fear. This result was so powerful that the cities of the Philistines came to reject the presence of the Ark, for fear that God's wrath would come upon them. Sadly, this fear was not one unto belief, but did generate respect for the God of Israel. Our God is not one to be messed with. His Word is true and meant to be obeyed. His salvation is by grace through faith in Jesus Christ, and must be accepted, for the forgiveness of sins. His commands are not options, but declarations that have negative consequences, if we choose to reject them. Do you fear the Lord? Do you respect and venerate Him above everything else in this Universe? Do you work to read, study, and obey His Word? Have you seen His hand of blessing and/or chastisement in your life? How have you shown God that you respect Him recently?

____

____

____

____

____

Write down one or more of the above applications that spoke to you personally, and pray that God will help you with it. If you have questions (or need help with application), please speak with your pastor/teacher:

____

____

____

Read I Samuel 6:1-21: The Philistines Return the Ark

1. How long was the Ark of the Covenant in the land of the Philistines (*v.1*)? _________________

2. Who did the Philistines call for, to receive counsel about the Ark (*v.2*)?

____

3. What did these men tell the Philistines to put with the Ark (*v.3*)?

____

4. When they did this, what did they say would happen (*v.3*)?

____

5. What were the Philistines told to give as an offering (*v.4*)?

____

6. What nation hardened their hearts against God, when He wrought wonderfully among them (*v.6*)?

____

7. Where were the Philistines told to lay the Ark (*v.7-8*)? _________________________

8. How would they know if the hand of God had smitten them (*v.9*)?

____

9. Did the Philistines obey their advisors (*v.10-11*)? _________________________

10. Where did the kine travel (*v.12*)?

____

11. What happened, when the men of Bethshemesh saw the cart with the Ark (*v.13*)?

____

12. What did they offer to the Lord out of the cart and kine (*v.14-15*)?

____

13. When the Philistines saw these things, what did they do (*v.16*)?

____

14. What did God do to the men of Bethshemesh (*v.19*)?_________________________

15. Why (*v.19*)? ____

16. Where did they send to, with hopes of getting rid of the Ark (*v.21*)? _______________________

<u>Applications</u>:

1. The Philistines sent the Ark back to Israel with a trespass offering. This offering was to apologize to the God of Heaven and seek His mercy. In response, God healed the smitten Philistines. There are times that we sin against God and need to apologize. Thankfully, God has provided sure means of restoration for the erring child. All we must do is repent of the sin and ask for forgiveness (*I John 1:9*). Do you keep short accounts of sin in your life? Have you ever had to tell God that you were sorry, and repent of sin? What sin are you struggling with right now, and praying that God will give you the victory over?

____

____

____

2. The men of Bethshemesh proved they did not want to obey God's Word. Instead, they wanted to do things their way, so they peered into the Ark of the Covenant, which was expressly forbidden. Because of their sin, God killed over fifty thousand people! Sin is rebellion against God's Word. It is serious and has far-reaching consequences: much more than we can ever understand. God wants us to be a people that obey Him and His Word, not ones that play around with sin. Is sin a serious thing to you, or is there something in your life that you are playing around with? If the latter, what is it? Will you pray that God will help you to repent of that sin?

____

____

____

____

Write down one or more of the above applications that spoke to you personally, and pray that God will help you with it. If you have questions (or need help with application), please speak with your pastor/teacher:

____

____

____

Read I Samuel 7:1-17: Samuel Encourages Israel to Return to God

1. Who came to take the Ark of the Covenant (*v.1*)? _______________________________________

2. Where did they bring it to (*v.1*)?_______________________________________

3. How long did the Ark abide there (*v.2*)?_______________________________________

4. What did God promise to do for Israel, if they stopped their idolatrous ways (*v.3*)?

____

5. Did Israel obey the voice of the Lord (*v.4*)? _______________________________________

6. What did Samuel promise to do for Israel (*v.5*)? _______________________________________

7. What did Israel confess that they had done (*v.6*)?_______________________________________

8. Who came up against Israel at Mizpah (*v.7*)?_______________________________________

9. What did Israel ask Samuel to do for them (*v.8*)?

____

10. What happened, when Samuel prayed for Israel (*v.9*)?

____

11. What did the Lord bring to discomfit the Philistines in battle (*v.10*)?

____

12. What did Samuel call the stone that he set up between Mizpeh and Shen (*v.12*)?_______________

13. Why (*v.12*)?_______________________________________

14. What happened with the cities that the Philistines had taken from Israel (*v.14*)?

____

15. For how long did Samuel judge Israel (*v.15*)?_______________________________________

16. Where was Samuel's home (*v.17*)?_______________________________________

<u>**Applications**</u>:

1. Israel knew that Samuel was a true prophet, a man of God. They believed that, if Samuel prayed for them, they would have their prayers answered. So, when the Philistines came up against them, they begged Samuel to keep praying for them. Do you know someone that prays, and God answers their prayers? Who are they, and how does that affect you? Do you have a desire to have that sort of relationship with God for yourself? What is the last prayer that God answered for you? What prayers are you praying for on a daily basis right now?

____

____

____

____

____

2. After God gave Israel the victory, Samuel raised a pillar in testimony to Him. This was not an idol, but a simple way of giving God the glory. When God answers our prayers, we ought to thank Him, as He so greatly deserves. What answers to prayer has God given you recently? Have you thanked Him for the answer? Have you publically testified to the church family and others as to what He has done for you? We ought to do this, and often. He deserves it.

____

____

____

____

Write down one or more of the above applications that spoke to you personally, and pray that God will help you with it. If you have questions (or need help with application), please speak with your pastor/teacher:

____

____

____

Read I Samuel 8:1-22: Israel Desires a King

1. When Samuel was old, who did he make to be judges over Israel (*v.1*)? _______________________

2. Did Samuel's sons follow after his ways (*v.3*)? _______________________________________

3. How did they differ from their father (*v.3*)?

____

4. Who called Samuel, to speak about the matter (*v.4*)?

____

5. Because of his age, and the actions of his sons, what did these people want Samuel to do (*v.5*)?

____

6. How did Samuel react to this (*v.6*)? _______________________________________

7. When Samuel prayed to God about the matter, who did the Lord say that Israel was rejecting (*v.7*)?

____

8. What did God tell Samuel to do about the matter (*v.9*)?

____

9. What are some of the things that Samuel said the king would do to Israel's sons (*v.11-12*)?

____

10. What are some of the things that he said the king would do to Israel's daughters (*v.13*)?

____

11. What are some of the things that Samuel said the king would take from Israel (*v.14-17*)?

____

12. What did he promise that Israel would eventually do, because of their king (*v.18*)? _______________

13. What did God promise to do, when Israel did this (*v.18*)?_______________________________

14. Despite Samuel's words, what did the people say in response (*v.19*)?

____

15. Who did Israel want to be like (*v.20*)? _______________________________________

<u>**Applications**</u>:

1. Sadly, Samuel fell into the trap that Eli did: he did not train his children to follow after the Lord. Not only did he not train them, but he allowed them to serve in a capacity of leadership and ministry, where they corrupted their office. God is very serious about parents training their children to follow Him. If you have children, are you training them to follow Christ? Have you given them the Gospel? Do you pray for their soul and future? If you do not have children, will you determine to train them to follow Christ, should God bless you with some in the future?

____

____

2. Israel desired a king, instead of Samuel being their judge. When Samuel began to take this personally, God reminded him that the people had not rejected the prophet, but God's leadership. Many people would rather follow after a human being than the God of the Bible. It is part of our sinful nature. Which do you prefer: obeying God and His Word, or obeying the whims of a human being? Why do you believe that it is important to obey this person/people? Why are they worthy of your obedience?

____

____

____

3. Samuel worked hard to try to dissuade Israel from demanding a king. He mentioned that they were rejecting God, in having this desire, and gave them many negative factors that would come with having a king. Nevertheless, because Israel rejected God and His Word, Samuel's words fell on deaf ears. Sin causes insanity. A person determined to sin cannot be reasoned with by logic or Scripture. Only God can open their ears and soften their hearts. The individual has to want to learn and follow Truth. Which type of person are you? Are you determined to do things your own way, or do you seek God's wisdom through His Word? Are you one that wants to follow your own path, or do you seek God's will for your life? Do you seek Truth, to follow it, or are you dead-set on doing what your flesh wants to do?

____

____

____

Write down one or more of the above applications that spoke to you personally, and pray that God will help you with it. If you have questions (or need help with application), please speak with your pastor/teacher:

____

____

Read I Samuel 9:1-27: God Calls Saul to Be King

1. What was notable about the man Kish (*v.1*)?_______________________________________

2. What was the name of this man's son (*v.2*)? ______________________________________

3. What did Kish lose (*v.3*)? ____

4. When they came to Zuph, who did Saul's servant say was there (*v.6*)? ________________

5. What was said about this person (*v.6*)?

____

____

6. What did the group have to give to the man of God for his help (*v.8*)?

____

7. Before they were called prophets, what were these men called (*v.9*)?_________________

8. A day before Saul came, what had God promised to send to Samuel (*v.16*)?

____

9. What was Samuel to do to this man (*v.16*)?

____

10. What was this man to do for Israel (*v.16*)?

____

11. Who did God say was the man that He spoke of (*v.17*)? _________________________

12. What did Samuel say was the fate of the missing asses (*v.20*)?____________________

13. How many people were eating with Saul and Samuel (*v.22*)? _____________________

14. What portion of meat was given to Saul (*v.24*)? ______________________________

15. Who was sent ahead of Saul, so that he and Samuel could speak alone (*v.27*)?

____

<u>**Applications**</u>:

1. Kish's donkeys became lost, so Saul willingly went to find them. This shows us the man's obedience to his father, as he contributed to the welfare of the family. In our day, many children are not made to contribute to their family. Instead, they are allowed to lay around the house and be lazy. How about you? Do you contribute to your family? How do you help out around the house? Would your parents call you lazy or hard-working? If you are a parent, are you teaching your children to contribute to the family, or are you allowing them to be lazy?

____

____

____

2. In addition to being a dutiful child, Saul did not give up on his quest, until a resolution presented itself. In our day, many people start what they do not finish. People start working on projects, reading books, and learning at school/college, but leave their work unfinished. God wants us to finish what we start. Are you a person that leaves things unfinished, or one that finishes what they start? Give an example of when you started something and saw it through to the end. Are you a person that wants to run the Christian race with patience, unto the finish line, or will you quit, when the going gets tough?

____

____

____

Write down one or more of the above applications that spoke to you personally, and pray that God will help you with it. If you have questions (or need help with application), please speak with your pastor/teacher:

____

____

____

Read I Samuel 10:1-27: Saul Is Crowned King

1. What did Samuel anoint Saul to be (*v.1*)? ____

2. Who did he say would meet him near Rachel's sepulcher (*v.2*)? _______________________________

3. What would they tell Saul (*v.2*)?

____

____

4. Who did Samuel say would meet Saul at the plain of Tabor (*v.3*)? ____________________________

5. What would they give him (*v.4*)? ____

6. Who did Samuel say that Saul would meet near the garrison of the Philistines (*v.5*)?

____

7. What special things would happen to Saul at that time (*v.6*)?

____

____

8. Where did Samuel then tell Saul that he would tarry for seven days (*v.8*)? ____________________

9. What happened to Saul, after he left Samuel (*v.9*)? _______________________________________

10. What did he do with the prophets (*v.10*)? ____

11. What proverb came from this occasion (*v.12*)? ____

12. To where did Samuel call Israel together (*v.17*)? _______________________________________

13. What did God tell Israel that they had done to Him (*v.19*)? _______________________________

14. Where did the Lord tell Samuel that Saul was hiding (*v.22*)? ______________________________

15. How tall was Saul (*v.23*)? ____

16. What did the people cry, when Samuel declared Saul to be God's chosen (*v.24*)?

____

<u>**Applications**</u>:

1. After Samuel anointed Saul to be the king of Israel, he gave him some signs to look for, to build his faith. Because Samuel was a true prophet of God, each one of these signs came to pass, and Saul was, no doubt, encouraged. We need things like that sometimes. We should not be a people that constantly seek signs from God before we obey Him. However, He sometimes sends various encouragements our way, to bolster our faith. Has God ever done this for you? How has He encouraged you recently: showing you that He cares about, and will take care of you?

____

____

____

2. Saul was not a prophet, but God sent His Spirit to allow the man to prophesy as one. This was a subtle reminder to Saul that he was not able to be a king, but God would help him to be a godly one. The same goes for any person. We are not able to do our jobs, fulfill our roles, and/or minister well without God's help. We need the filling of the Spirit, to please Him. What is your God-given role right now? How do you trust in God to help you to fulfill this role? What do you believe God has for your future? What are your hopes and dreams? As you trust in God for your present, will you seek His help and guidance for your future?

____

____

3. Saul was the newly crowned King of Israel. However, some detractors publicly refused both his kingship and God's will. Instead of punishing these evil men, the new king had mercy and ignored them. Life is about picking our battles, with God's help. Many times, we need to ignore the detractors and leave their fate to the Lord. In fact, Jesus tells us that vengeance is His, not ours. When people hurt us, we must forgive, and let God judge. Do you believe this? Do you pick your battles, or do you have to win every one? Do you let people have the last word? Do you seek revenge and hold grudges, or allow God to be the Judge of the Universe? Write down some examples below.

____

____

____

Write down one or more of the above applications that spoke to you personally, and pray that God will help you with it. If you have questions (or need help with application), please speak with your pastor/teacher:

____

Read I Samuel 11:1-15: Saul's First Actions as King

1. Who came and encamped against Jabesh-gilead (*v.1*)?_______________________________________

2. What did the men of the city want this man to do with them (*v.1*)?

____

3. What condition did the Ammonite put forth to the men (*v.2*)?

____

4. Why did he want them to do this (*v.2*)? ____

5. How many days' respite did the men of the city ask for (*v.3*)? _____________________________

6. Who came to Saul (*v.4*)?____

7. How did the people react to the message (*v.4*)?

____

8. Who came upon Saul (*v.6*)? ____

9. What did he do with a yoke of oxen (*v.7*)?

____

____

10. Because of Saul's message, how did the people of Israel react (*v.7*)?

____

11. How many men of Israel and Judah came out to him (*v.8*)? _____________________________

12. When did Saul say that the men of Jabesh-gilead would have help (*v.9*)?

____

13. How did they respond to the message (*v.9*)?____

14. Why did Saul not allow the people to kill the detractors for him (*v.13*)?

____

15. Where did the people go to renew the kingdom (*v.14-15*)? ______________________________

<u>**Applications**</u>:

1. Saul's kingship was very tenuous due to the people that opposed him, and his reaction to them. To encourage the new king, and prove God's choice to the people, the Lord granted a tremendous victory over the Ammonites. A perilous situation was turned into a miraculous one! God put His Spirit upon the new king and provided an impossible victory! He used this to solidify the kingdom for Saul. Has God ever given you an impossible victory? Has He ever answered an impossible prayer for you? Did you give Him the glory for it? Did it encourage you and others? What impossible things has God done for you?

____

____

____

____

____

2. Saul's victory was so great in the eyes of the people that they wanted to bring out the detractors that previously opposed him, and kill them! Saul wisely refused such desires, and reminded them that the victory given that day was of the Lord. People like to worship other people. They also like to give those same people the glory, and raise them up on pedestals. As God's people, when others praise us, we need to be careful to give God the glory. Any good thing that comes out of our lives is because of Christ. Any victory or great thing is from His power and ability. When someone praises you, do you give God the glory? Instead of gaining a large ego and becoming prideful, do you quickly remind yourself to be humble, because God works through you? Name an instance where this happened recently.

____

____

____

____

____

Write down one or more of the above applications that spoke to you personally, and pray that God will help you with it. If you have questions (or need help with application), please speak with your pastor/teacher:

____

____

____

Read I Samuel 12:1-25: Samuel Charges Israel

1. What two things did Samuel tell Israel that he had done for them (*v.1*)?

____

2. What did Israel have to say about Samuel's testimony of ministry toward them (*v.4*)?

____

____

3. Who did Samuel say was witness against Israel (*v.5*)? ___________________________

4. Who did he say advanced Moses and Aaron, and delivered Israel from Egypt (*v.6*)? ___________

5. Who did God send to bring Israel out of Egypt (*v.8*)?___________________________

6. Why did God sell Israel into the hands of their enemies (*v.9*)?

____

7. Who did He send to deliver Israel out of the hands of their enemies (*v.11*)?

____

8. When Israel was opposed by the Ammonites, what did they say to Samuel (*v.12*)?

____

9. Why was this an affront to Samuel and God (*v.12*)?

____

10. What did Samuel promise would happen to the people, if they rebelled against God (*v.15*)?

____

11. Why did Samuel give the people the sign of thunder and lightning (*v.17*)?

____

12. How did they respond to this sign (*v.18*)?

____

13. How did Samuel say that they should serve the Lord (*v.20*)? ___________________________

14. What did he promise to not stop doing for Israel (*v.23*)? ___________________________

<u>**Applications**</u>:

1. Samuel may not have raised his children to follow the Lord, but he was a godly prophet. He never stole from or cheated anyone. He never took a bribe, to corrupt judgment. Samuel was an ethical man. When asked about these things, Israel even agreed to this testimony. God's people ought to be known as ethical, godly individuals, especially the spiritual leaders. What is your testimony with others? Do they know you as honest and ethical? What about your spiritual leaders? Are they honest and ethical?

____

____

2. Again, Samuel made sure that Israel was fully aware of the error they were making in turning away from God's will for their government. They rejected God as their king, and turned to a man. Whenever we do this, we err. Who is the king of your life? Is it God or Man? What is your source of instruction? What is the foundation for your living? Do you defer to God's Word, or to Man's teachings?

____

____

____

3. After giving his speech and God sending confirming signs, Samuel promised to never stop praying for the children of Israel. In fact, he promised to continue to teach them the scriptures (the good and right way). Samuel grieved that Israel was turning away from God, but did not stop praying and teaching (which would have been sin for him). Do you pray for people that have turned away from God? Despite their unbelief, do you continue to live for Christ and teach His Word, when able? Who are you praying for right now that needs to get right with God?

____

____

____

Write down one or more of the above applications that spoke to you personally, and pray that God will help you with it. If you have questions (or need help with application), please speak with your pastor/teacher:

____

____

____

Read I Samuel 13:1-23: God Rejects Saul

1. After reigning for two years, how many men did Saul choose out, to be with him (*v.2*)?

____

2. What did Jonathan smite with his men in Geba (*v.3*)?

____

3. Who came to fight against Israel at Michmash (*v.5*)? _______________________________________

4. How did Israel respond (*v.6*)? ____

5. How long had Samuel told Saul to wait for him (*v.8*)? _______________________________

6. What did Saul tell the people to bring to him (*v.9*)?

____

7. What did he offer (*v.9*)? ____

8. Who came, as soon as Saul had finished (*v.10*)? _______________________________________

9. What did Samuel ask Saul (*v.11*)? ____

10. Who did Saul blame for his transgression (*v.11*)? _______________________________________

11. How did Samuel respond to Saul's excuses (*v.13*)? _______________________________________

12. What did he have to say about Saul's kingdom (*v.14*)? _______________________________

13. What sort of king did God look for (*v.14*)?

____

14. What was not found in all of Israel (*v.19*)? _______________________________________

15. What was not found in the hand of any of the people that went to the battle (*v.22*)?

____

<u>**Applications**</u>:

1. Samuel was late for his appointment with Saul. Because of this, Saul felt that he need to go outside of God's Law, and perform a sacrifice himself (which was expressly forbidden). Saul's lack of patience got the better of him, and he paid the price for it. As believers in Jesus Christ, we need to learn to adhere to God's timetable, not our own. This requires learning patience. Sometimes, God delays an answer to prayer or blessing just to see if we will continue to be faithful and wait on Him. Are you a patient person? Not many people are. In fact, in our society, patience is become more and more rare. Will you work on your patience? In what ways can you learn to be more patient, to please the Lord?

____

____

____

____

2. Saul not only went outside of God's boundaries, because of his lack of patience, but also refused to take the blame for his actions. Instead, he blamed the people, Samuel, and the situation that he was in. Saul could have repented and asked forgiveness, but we see none of that here. This is born of pride. As believers, it falls to us to humble ourselves before God and His Word. Sometimes, this means admitting when we are wrong and repenting of sin. Do you ever admit that you are wrong, when you have sinned against God or someone else? Do you ever say that you are sorry and ask for forgiveness? When was the last time that you did this?

____

____

____

____

Write down one or more of the above applications that spoke to you personally, and pray that God will help you with it. If you have questions (or need help with application), please speak with your pastor/teacher:

____

____

____

<u>Read I Samuel 14:1-22: Jonathan Defeats the Philistines</u>

1. To where did Jonathan bring his armor-bearer (**v.1**)?

____

2. Who did he neglect to tell about his departure (**v.1**)? _______________________________

3. Where did Saul tarry (**v.2**)? ____

4. About how many men were with him (**v.2**)? _______________________________

5. Who was the Lord's priest in Shiloh, during this time (**v.3**)? _______________________

6. What were the names of the two rocks that Jonathan passed between (**v.4**)?

____

7. What were the names of the two cities that these rocks were situated against (**v.5**)?

____

8. Why did Jonathan believe that God could work with them against the Philistines (**v.6**)?

____

9. Did the armor-bearer want to go with Jonathan, or was he afraid (**v.7**)?

____

10. What sign did Jonathan look for, where he would know that God would be with them (**v.8-10**)?

____

11. How did the Philistines respond, when Jonathan made themselves known to them (**v.12**)?

____

12. About how many men did Jonathan and his armor-bearer kill (**v.14**)? _______________

13. How did the Philistines respond to this great victory (**v.15**)?

____

14. What did Saul's watchmen see the Philistines doing to one another (**v.16**)?

____

15. Who could Saul not find among their people (**v.17**)?_______________________________

16. What did Saul tell Ahiah to bring to him (*v.18*)?_______________________________________

17. When Saul and his army came to the battle, what did they find (*v.20*)?

____

18. How did the traitorous Hebrews respond to what was happening to the Philistines (*v.21*)?

____

19. How did the cowardly Hebrews respond to this event (*v.22*)?

____

Applications:

1. In this chapter, God used Jonathan in a miraculous way, but he forgot to do something very important: he did not tell his father that he was departing from the camp. Good communication is vital in any healthy relationship. Many marriages, families, workplaces, and churches both thrive and suffer, because of the good communication (or lack thereof) between those involved. Do you communicate well in your relationships? If you are married, do you communicate well with your spouse? If you have children, or are a child, does your family communicate well? In what ways do you need to work on your communication skills?

____

____

2. Jonathan sought a sign from God, and acted on faith based upon the answer. God has given us His Word to obey and prove. We do not seek signs, but prove the truth of the Bible! What promise has God showed you lately, in the Word, that you need to prove Him on? How will you do this?

____

____

____

Write down one or more of the above applications that spoke to you personally, and pray that God will help you with it. If you have questions (or need help with application), please speak with your pastor/teacher:

____

____

____

Read I Samuel 14:23-52: Saul's Foolish Oath

1. Who saved Israel, when they fought against the Philistines (*v.23*)? _______________________

2. Despite the great victory that day, why were the men of Israel distressed (*v.24*)?

____

____

3. When the men came into a wood, what was on the ground (*v.25*)? _______________________

4. What did Jonathan do, when he saw this (*v.27*)?

____

5. What happened to him, when he did this (*v.27*)? _______________________

6. Because of Saul's oath, what was the state of the people (*v.28*)? _______________________

7. What did Jonathan have to say about his father's oath (*v.29*)?

____

8. After hearing Jonathan's words, what did the people do (*v.32*)?

____

9. How did they eat these animals (*v.32*)? _______________________

10. To avoid sinning against God, what did Saul tell the people to do (*v.34*)?

____

11. When Saul wanted to fight against the Philistines, what did the priest request (*v.36*)?

____

12. After they prayed, what was God's reaction (*v.37*)? _______________________

13. What did Saul determine to do to Jonathan, because of his actions (*v.39*)? _______________________

14. How did the people react to this proclamation (*v.39*)?

____

15. After casting lots and accusing Jonathan, how did the people respond (*v.45*)?

____

16. What was the name of Saul's wife (*v.50*)? _______________________________________

17. What did he do, when he found a strong or valiant man (*v.52*)?

____

<u>Applications</u>:

1. God tells us very clearly that He saved Israel that day, it was not Saul's power or skill. It was not the might of the Israeli army. It was God that saved Israel from the Philistines. Just so, we must recognize when God helps us, and give Him the glory. It is God that gives us our strength, skill, opportunities, and increase. Do you recognize this in your own life? When was the last time that God helped you? Did you give Him the glory?

____

____

____

2. Saul made a foolish oath that ended up hurting the children of Israel, and even threatened his own son's life! This oath was not made to please the Lord, but was one given out of pride. We need to be careful of the promises that we make: ensuring that they are biblical and not born of pride. What promises have you made to God? Are they biblical and attainable with God's help? How will this promise help you to become a better Christian?

____

____

____

Write down one or more of the above applications that spoke to you personally, and pray that God will help you with it. If you have questions (or need help with application), please speak with your pastor/teacher:

____

____

____

Read I Samuel 15:1-12: Saul Fails God Again

1. What did Amalek do to Israel, when he came up from Egypt (*v.2*)?

____

2. What did God order Saul to do to the Amalekites, because of this (*v.3*)?

____

3. How many people did Saul gather to do this (*v.4*)? _________________________________

4. When Saul came to a city of Amalek, what did he do (*v.5*)? _______________________

5. Who did he tell to depart from the Amalekites (*v.6*)? ____________________________

6. Why did Saul spare their lives (*v.6*)?

____

7. Who did Saul spare of the Amalekites (*v.8*)? ____________________________________

8. What else did he spare (*v.9*)?

____

9. What did they destroy utterly (*v.9*)? ____

10. What did God have to say to Samuel about Saul's actions (*v.11*)?

____

11. Why did God feel this way about Saul (*v.11*)?

____

12. How did Samuel respond (*v.11*)? ____

Applications:

1. The Amalekites were an ungodly group of people that fought against Israel, when they came out from Egypt. Because of their actions, God promised that He would wipe them out. This promise took several hundred years to come to fruition, but did come to pass. Through this event, we understand that God keeps His promises, on His timetable. Therefore, we need to learn to be patient and trust Him. What promise has God shown to you, in His Word, recently? Will you trust Him to keep His promises?

____

____

2. The instance with the Amalekites also shows us that God sees everything, and no one gets away with anything. At times, it seems like the world gets away with its wickedness. This has been a perceived problem for many thousands of years. The truth is that no one gets away with anything. The wicked that seemingly flourish on the earth will be judged for eternity (unless they turn to Christ). Just so, the believer that does wickedly is guaranteed chastisement by their Father in Heaven. Do you believe that God is in control? Do you believe that no one gets away with anything? How have you observed these truths in the world?

____

____

____

____

3. God told Saul to destroy everything and everyone belonging to the Amalekites, but the king thought that he knew what was best. Because of his prideful actions, God regretted ever choosing Saul to be king. When God told Saul to destroy everything, He meant to destroy *everything*. In other words, God means what He says. When God says that salvation is through Christ alone, He means what He says. When He says that we cannot be Christ's disciples, unless we love Him above all, He means what He says. Do you believe that God means what He says, in His Word, or do you ignore/try to spin Scripture?

____

____

Write down one or more of the above applications that spoke to you personally, and pray that God will help you with it. If you have questions (or need help with application), please speak with your pastor/teacher:

____

____

____

1. When Samuel came to Saul, what did Saul declare (*v.13*)?

____

2. How did Samuel reply (*v.14*)?

____

3. What was Saul's excuse (*v.15*)?

____

4. When did God make Saul to be the head of the tribes of Israel (*v.17*)?

____

5. What had He told Saul to do to the Amalekites (*v.18*)?

____

6. What did Samuel accuse Saul of doing (*v.19*)?

____

7. What did Saul stubbornly proclaim about his actions (*v.20*)?

____

8. Who did he blame for taking the spoil (*v.21*)? _______________________________________

9. What does God say is better than sacrifice (*v.22*)? _______________________________________

10. What does He see rebellion and stubbornness as (*v.23*)?

____

11. What did Saul want Samuel to do with him (*v.25*)?

____

12. Because Samuel would not do this, what did Saul do (*v.27*)?

____

13. When this happened, what did Samuel declare (*v.28*)?

____

<u>**Applications**</u>:

1. Saul was chosen to be king of Israel, when he was little in his own sight. In other words, God chose Saul, because he was humble. Saul understood that he could not be a good king without God's help. However, he eventually decided that he knew better than God: becoming proud. It takes work to be humble. The believer that pleases God must humble themselves before God and His Word daily. We must understand that we cannot live a life pleasing to the Lord without His help. The day that we start to think that we know better than God is a sorry one. What about you? Do you work to be humble? Do you work to obey the Word of God, or think that you know better than Him?

____

____

2. When Saul's sin was called out by Samuel, instead of admitting to it, he made several mistakes. One was that he refused to acknowledge his sin. Saul stubbornly maintained his perceived righteousness, by making the excuse of reserving animals for sacrifice. Samuel's rebuff was that obeying God's Word was better than sacrifice. Many people today believe that they are worshipping God, because they do good things in His name. However, if they do not obey the Word in doing those good things, God does not accept it. Do you believe that obeying God's Word is better than sacrificing your goods to Him? Do you understand that God wants your heart, not your money, goods, etc? Does He have your heart right now? If not, will you surrender to Him?

____

____

3. Saul's second mistake was blaming the sin on someone else. Instead of blaming himself, he chose to blame the people for his sin. Pride tells us that we are perfect, when we are not. It makes us to excuse our sin, when we must take responsibility for our actions. We live in a world that likes to blame others, instead of being responsible. How about you? When your sin is found out, do you admit and repent of it, or do you try to blame others?

____

____

Write down one or more of the above applications that spoke to you personally, and pray that God will help you with it. If you have questions (or need help with application), please speak with your pastor/teacher:

____

____

____

Read I Samuel 16:1-23: God Chooses David as King

1. What did God ask Samuel about Saul (*v.1*)?

____

2. What did He tell him to do (*v.1*)? _______________________________________

3. Why (*v.1*)? ____

4. What was Samuel afraid that Saul would do to him (*v.2*)? __________________________

5. What did God tell him to do (*v.2*)?

____

6. What did the elders of the town ask Samuel, when he came to Bethlehem (*v.4*)?

____

7. Who did Samuel call to the sacrifice (*v.5*)?______________________________________

8. What did God tell Samuel not to base his judgment upon (*v.7*)?

____

9. What did He say that He looked upon, when judging a person (*v.7*)?__________________

10. How many of Jesse's sons passed before Samuel and were rejected (*v.10*)? ______________

11. Where was Jesse's youngest son (*v.11*)? ______________________________________

12. Who did Samuel anoint to be the king of Israel (*v.13*)? ________________________

13. Who came upon this man, but departed from Saul (*v.13-14*)? ____________________

14. Who was sent to come before Saul and play on the harp (*v.19-23*)? ________________

<u>**Applications**</u>:

1. God makes a tremendous statement in this passage: Man looks on the outward appearance, but God looks upon the heart. Mankind likes to judge based upon perceived circumstances and outward appearances. Our flesh likes to judge the book by its cover, without reading the book! However, our God cares about our heart, not so much our outward appearance. The apostles even tell the women of the churches this in their epistles! We need to be careful to care for our hearts. Do you care more for your outward appearance, or your heart? Do you take time every day to work on your walk with God? Do you judge people by how they look, or how they line up with God's Word?

____

____

2. When David was anointed to be king of Israel, the Spirit of God came upon him. Just so, the Spirit left Saul, and an evil spirit came to trouble him. Literally, Saul was being oppressed by this evil spirit, and made to become terrified and paranoid. The only cure for this torment, was the playing of the harp. No doubt, David would come and play some of his psalms, to help soothe the troubled king. God-honoring music (hymns and psalms played and/or sung with an orchestra/piano/acapella) goes a long way to helping our troubled hearts. If we are being oppressed by an evil spirit, this sort of music (along with Bible reading and prayer), can cast it away. Have you ever been oppressed by an evil spirit? Have you ever become angry, worried, afraid, and/or paranoid for no good reason? When this happens, we must flee to the Word, prayer, and God-honoring music. Do you have a source for such music? What is it? If you do not know where to find God-honoring music, will you talk to your pastor/teacher about it?

____

____

____

____

Write down one or more of the above applications that spoke to you personally, and pray that God will help you with it. If you have questions (or need help with application), please speak with your pastor/teacher:

____

____

____

<u>Read I Samuel 17:1-18: Goliath Challenges Israel</u>

1. Where did Saul and his army pitch against the Philistines (*v.2*)?_______________________________

2. What was the name of the champion that went out from the Philistines (*v.4*)?_______________________

3. How tall was this man (*v.4*)?____

4. What was the staff of his spear like (*v.7*)? ____

5. What did the man want Israel to do (*v.8*)?

____

6. What did he say that the Philistines would do, if Israel's champion could kill him (*v.9*)?

____

7. What did Goliath say that Israel would do, if he killed Israel's champion (*v.9*)?

____

8. How did Saul and all Israel respond to the words of Goliath (*v.11*)?

____

9. Who was David the son of (*v.12*)? ____

10. Which of David's brothers had followed Saul to the battle (*v.13*)?

____

11. For how many days did Goliath present himself to Israel (*v.16*)? _________________________________

12. What did Jesse want David to take to the war camp (*v.17-18*)?

____

13. What did he want David to do, while he was there (*v.18*)?

____

<u>**Applications**</u>:

1. Saul had turned God's people into a faithless group of individuals, because of his pride. This means that they trusted in their strength and skill, instead of looking to God for help. Goliath challenged the armies of Israel for forty days, and Israel's faithless reaction makes this truth very apparent. When we live in the flesh, we become faithless, especially in the face of impossible odds. What about you? Do you trust in your strength and skill, or do you trust in God's? What about in the face of impossible odds? Will you work to trust in the Lord to help you: keeping you safe, providing for your needs, giving you wisdom, or providing whatever else you need? What do you need to trust Him with right now?

____

____

____

2. David was a dutiful son. He returned from helping to relieve Saul's paranoia, to help his father with his flocks. When Jesse needed his son to travel to the battle front, to deliver food and check on his siblings, he went without argument or hesitation. Do you help out in your family? Do you honor and obey your parents? How did you help contribute to your household this week?

____

____

____

____

Write down one or more of the above applications that spoke to you personally, and pray that God will help you with it. If you have questions (or need help with application), please speak with your pastor/teacher:

____

____

____

Read I Samuel 17:19-37: David and Goliath

1. Who were Saul and his men fighting, in the Valley of Elah (*v.19*)? _______________________________

2. As David spoke with his brothers, who came out of the Philistine army (*v.23*)? _________________

3. When the men of Israel saw the man, what was their response (*v.24*)? _______________________

4. What was promised to the man that would kill Goliath (*v.25*)?

____

____

5. Who became angry against David (*v.28*)? ____

6. Why did he say that David came to the battle (*v.28*)?

____

7. What was David's response (*v.29*)? ____

8. Who heard of David's words (*v.31*)? ____

9. What did David tell Saul that he would do (*v.32*)? ____

10. Why did Saul tell David that he could not go into battle (*v.33*)?

____

11. What two animals did God help David kill, to protect his flock (*v.34-37*)?

____

Applications:

1. The armies of Israel were afraid, as was their king. However, a young man named David had faith in the God of Israel. When David spoke out, he was ridiculed and doubted by "God's people". Nonetheless, there was a cause: glorifying God. What would you do, if this was you? Would you give in to the naysayers and doubters, or continue to trust in the Lord God? Has there been a time where your faith has been ridiculed? When was this? How did you respond?

2. Saul told David that he was not able to go against Goliath. David had everything going against him: his own family, nation, and king doubted him. In addition, he was a young man going against a trained warrior! Every part of this scenario went against David and for Goliath. But, David had one thing going in his favor: his faith in God, and this alone nullified any opposition. Saul was right, David was not able on his own. But, with God all things are possible. Do you understand that you are not able to live a life pleasing to God? Do you believe that you can live such a life with God's help? In what ways do you need God's help to overcome life's obstacles?

____

____

____

____

3. David believed that he could fight the giant based upon what God had helped him to do in the past. The young man had miraculously been able to kill both a lion and bear, to protect his sheep. If God could do that, then there was no doubt that He could help David defeat the giant. God answers prayer and blesses obedience, to build our faith in Him (which strengthens our relationship with Him). How is your faith life? Is your faith in God stronger today than last year? What about three years ago? Five? Ten? What has God done recently that has strengthened your faith?

____

____

____

____

Write down one or more of the above applications that spoke to you personally, and pray that God will help you with it. If you have questions (or need help with application), please speak with your pastor/teacher:

____

____

____

Read I Samuel 17:38-58: David and Goliath (Part Two)

1. Why could David not wear Saul's armor (*v.39*)?_______________________________________

2. What did he take into battle instead (*v.40*)?

____

3. When David came near to Goliath, what did the giant do (*v.43*)?

____

4. What did David say that Goliath came against him with (*v.45*)?

____

5. What did he say that he came against Goliath with (*v.45*)?

____

6. Why did David say that God would deliver Goliath into his hand (*v.46*)?

____

7. Why else (*v.47*)?

____

____

8. What happened, when David slang the stone at Goliath (*v.49*)?

____

9. What happened, when the Philistines saw David's victory (*v.51*)? ___________________________

10. How far did Israel pursue the Philistines (*v.52*)?

____

11. Where did David put Goliath's armor (*v.54*)?_______________________________________

12. Whose son was David (*v.58*)? ____

<u>**Applications**</u>:

1. David went against Goliath, so that the people in the surrounding camps, and all the earth, would know that there was a God in Israel. Philistia mocked the Jews. Israel lost faith in their God. But, David had not, and wanted his brethren to trust in God anew. The young man was not looking for glory and power for himself. Instead, he wanted to glorify God. You may be the only person in your family, workplace, or church living for God right now. Will you continue to live for Him? Will you do so, to glorify and point others to Him? How can you do this, given your current circumstances?

____

____

____

____

2. David also went against Goliath, so that the people of Israel would know that the battle was the Lord's. As human beings, we like to get caught up in our own pride. We like to believe that it is our skill, strength, and wealth that wins battles. The truth is that God alone gives us what we need to win the day, if He desires so. We live and serve at His pleasure. Do you believe this? How do you fight your battles? Do you open your mouth and flex your muscles, or do you pray and trust God to work everything together for good? How has God provided for and delivered you recently?

____

____

____

Write down one or more of the above applications that spoke to you personally, and pray that God will help you with it. If you have questions (or need help with application), please speak with your pastor/teacher:

____

____

____

Read I Samuel 18:1-16: Saul Becomes Jealous of David

1. Whose soul did David's become knit with (*v.1*)? _______________________________

2. What did David and Jonathan make with one another (*v.3*)? _______________________________

3. How did David behave himself before Saul (*v.5*)? _______________________________

4. What did the women of the cities of Israel sing about Saul and David (*v.7*)?

____

5. How did Saul react to this (*v.8*)? _______________________________

6. What did he do with David from that time forward (*v.9*)?_______________________________

7. What happened to Saul, when the evil spirit came upon him the next day (*v.10*)?

____

8. What was in his hand (*v.10*)? _______________________________

9. Who did Saul try to kill with this weapon (*v.11*)?_______________________________

10. Why did he become afraid of David (*v.12*)? _______________________________

11. How did David continue to act before Saul (*v.14*)? _______________________________

12. Why (*v.14*)?_______________________________

13. How did Israel and Judah respond to David (*v.16*)? _______________________________

Applications:

1. When we are filled with the flesh, one definite fruit that comes forth is paranoia and jealousy. We see both of these coming from Saul, as he became jealous of David's achievements. A Spirit-filled Christian will not be jealous of the blessing that God brings about in someone's life, as they walk with Him. Instead, we will rejoice with and encourage them. How about you? Are you a jealous person? Do you rejoice with others, when God blesses them? Are you a good sport in competitions? How have you proved this recently? How do you need to work on this?

____

____

____

____

2. David behaved himself wisely, because the Lord was with him. The Lord was with him, because the man loved his God, and sought to obey Him. If we follow after Christ, we are guaranteed God's presence about us (whether we feel it or not). One proof of God's presence is behaving ourselves wisely and properly before others. Have you ever seen God bless your work, as you walk with Him? Have you ever seen Him help you to behave properly before others in a miraculous way? How has God helped you in these ways?

____

____

____

____

Write down one or more of the above applications that spoke to you personally, and pray that God will help you with it. If you have questions (or need help with application), please speak with your pastor/teacher:

____

____

____

Read I Samuel 18:17-30: David Marries Saul's Daughter

1. Who did Saul want to give to David, to be his wife (*v.17*)? _______________________________

2. What prerequisite did Saul have for this marriage (*v.17*)?

____

3. When Saul's daughter should have been given to David, who did Saul give her to (*v.19*)?

____

4. Which of Saul's daughters loved David (*v.20*)?____

5. Why did Saul agree to give her to him (*v.21*)?

____

6. Why did David not think himself suitable to be the king's son-in-law (*v.23*)?

____

7. Why did David kill two hundred of the Philistines (*v.27*)?

____

8. What did Saul perceive about David, because of his feat (*v.28*)?

____

9. How did he react to this truth (*v.29*)?

____

10. How did David behave himself against the Philistines (*v.30*)? _______________________________

Applications:

1. David was no fool. He knew that Saul was trying to kill him, but he was also humble. When Saul wanted him to marry his daughter, David put forth his unworthiness with humility. To prove himself to the king, God allowed him to have a mighty victory over the Philistines. What about you? Are you a humble person? Do you work at humility? Are you teachable, or do you try to tell everyone else how smart you are? God can only use and bless humble individuals.

____

____

____

2. David and his men went forth and slew two hundred Philistines, so that David could marry Saul's daughter. This made Saul even more afraid of the man, because he knew that God was with him: protecting and giving him victories. When we walk with God, He protects us. The only harm that ever comes to us is that which is allowed by His plan. It was not God's plan for David to be killed by Saul. Instead, David was to be king. Therefore, he was invincible in the will of God. Do you believe this? Is your God able to keep you safe, as you walk in His will? Does He fight your battles for you? When was a time that God divinely protected you?

____

____

____

____

Write down one or more of the above applications that spoke to you personally, and pray that God will help you with it. If you have questions (or need help with application), please speak with your pastor/teacher:

____

____

____

Read I Samuel 19:1-24: Saul Hunts David

1. What did Saul tell Jonathan and his servants (*v.1*)? ________________________________

2. Who told David about Saul's plan (*v.2*)?________________________________

3. Where did he tell him to go (*v.2*)? ________________________________

4. Why did Jonathan tell Saul that he should not seek to kill David (*v.4*)?

____

____

5. Did Saul listen to Jonathan (*v.6*)? ________________________________

6. After defeating the Philistines again, what came upon Saul (*v.9*)?

____

7. What did Saul seek to do to David, because of this (*v.10*)?

____

8. How did David escape from Saul (*v.12*)?

____

9. What did Michal put in David's bed, to pretend that he was there (*v.13*)?

____

10. What did she tell Saul's messengers (*v.14*)?________________________________

11. To where did David flee from Saul (*v.18*)? ________________________________

12. When Saul's messengers went to kill David, what happened to them (*v.20*)?

____

13. How many times did this happen (*v.21*)? ________________________________

14. When Saul went to kill David himself, what happened to him (*v.23-24*)?

____

<u>**Applications**</u>:

1. Jonathan was the very voice of reason with his father. This time, Saul listened to him, and restored David to his office (even if temporarily). Sometimes, people need to hear the truth, in order to do what is right. This does not mean that we be disrespectful to those in authority. We can be truthful, while being submissive. Are you a person that loves the truth? If someone close to you is sinning against someone else, do you speak up? When was a time that you stood up for the truth?

____

____

____

____

2. In this passage, Saul tried to kill David seven times, and God delivered him out of the king's hand each time. God is able to protect us, if He is willing. In David's case, He was willing, and so David was kept safe. Do you believe that God is able to keep you safe? How has He done this recently?

____

____

____

Write down one or more of the above applications that spoke to you personally, and pray that God will help you with it. If you have questions (or need help with application), please speak with your pastor/teacher:

____

____

____

Read I Samuel 20:1-23: David Flees from Saul

1. Did Jonathan think that Saul would hide his plans for David from him (**v.2**)? _______________________

2. Why did David believe that Saul was hiding his plans from Jonathan (**v.3**)?

____

3. What event was coming the next day (**v.5**)? ____

4. Where was Jonathan to say that David was, if Saul mentioned his absence (**v.6**)?

____

5. How would the two men know that David would have peace (**v.7**)?

____

6. What did David want Jonathan to do, if there was iniquity found in him (**v.8**)? _______________________

7. What did Jonathan ask David to do for his house (**v.14-15**)?

____

8. What did Jonathan make with the house of David (**v.16**)?_______________________________________

9. Why did he say that David would be missed (**v.18**)?

____

10. Where did Jonathan tell David to go and hide himself (**v.19**)?_______________________________

11. How many arrows did he say that he would shoot (**v.20**)? _________________________________

12. How would David know that he was in danger (**v.22**)?

____

Applications:

1. David and Jonathan were the best of friends. Even though Jonathan saw God's hand upon David's life, he was happy for his friend that God blessed and protected him. This is not only being a good friend, but a good Christian. Who are your good friends? Are they followers of Jesus Christ, or followers of the world's ways? Do they help you to be a better Christian, or tempt you to go the way of the world?

____

____

2. Because of their friendship, Jonathan and David made a covenant with each other, to protect it. True friends help each other through thick and thin. They encourage each other, pray for each other, and rejoice together. This is also seen as Jonathan speaks to Saul on David's behalf several times, even at the risk of his own life! As previously mentioned, who are your good friends? Do you help them through easy and hard times? Do you encourage them? Do you pray for them? Do you rejoice, when God blesses them? What are some examples of the love that you have for your friends?

____

____

____

____

Write down one or more of the above applications that spoke to you personally, and pray that God will help you with it. If you have questions (or need help with application), please speak with your pastor/teacher:

____

____

____

<u>Read I Samuel 20:24-42: David Flees from Saul (Part Two)</u>

1. Why did Saul believe David was absent on the first day of the feast (*v.26*)?

____

2. Who did Saul become angry against, because of David's absence (*v.30*)? _______________________

3. What did he say would happen, as long as David lived (*v.31*)?

____

4. What did Saul cast at Jonathan (*v.33*)?_______________________________________

5. What did Jonathan know about his father (*v.33*)?

____

6. Where did Jonathan say that he shot his arrows (*v.37*)? _______________________________

7. Who knew about the matter between David and Jonathan (*v.39*)?

____

8. Where did Jonathan have the lad take the arrows (*v.40*)? _______________________________

9. Once the lad left, who came out to Jonathan (*v.41*)? _______________________________

10. Who was between the covenant of David and Jonathan (*v.42*)?_______________________________

<u>Applications</u>:

1. Because of his rebelliousness against God, Saul went down a very bad road that became worse over time. Eventually, he got to the place where he became wrathful against his own son, to the point of trying to kill him! Imagine being given over to such hatred of someone, that they would try to kill their own child! Sadly, many people have anger problems, in our day. If left unchecked, this can manifest itself in many ways, and none of them good. Do you have anger problems? Do you harbor grudges against people, or lash out at others? Give some examples. If you have anger problems, will you determine to work on this, and ask God to help you with it, so that others do not suffer from your sin?

____

____

____

____

2. Jonathan knew that God had chosen David over him to be the king of Israel. Nevertheless, he knew that David was a righteous man, and God's choice. Instead of getting mad at God's will, he accepted it, and was happy for his friend. True godliness is surrendered to God's will, no matter what it is. Are you surrendered to God's will for your life? Are you willing to do whatever He would have you to do?

____

3. In relation to the previous application, we understand that true friends are happy for God's blessings upon each other. Are you a true friend? Are you happy, when God blesses your friends, or do you get jealous? Are you excited, when God works in their lives? When was a time when you were happy for something that God did for one of your friends?

____

____

____

Write down one or more of the above applications that spoke to you personally, and pray that God will help you with it. If you have questions (or need help with application), please speak with your pastor/teacher:

____

____

____

<u>**Read I Samuel 21:1-15: David Flees to the Philistines**</u>

1. To where did David flee from Saul (*v.1*)? ____

2. Who was there to meet him (*v.1*)?____

3. Why was this man afraid of David (*v.1*)?

____

4. What was David's reason for being alone (*v.2*)?

____

5. What did David ask Ahimelech for (*v.3*)? ___________________________________

6. What did Ahimelech give to David (*v.6*)? ___________________________________

7. Who was also at Nob (*v.7*)? ____

8. What did this man do for Saul (*v.7*)? ___________________________________

9. What else did David ask Ahimelech for (*v.8*)? _______________________________

10. What did the priest give to David (*v.9*)? _________________________________

11. Why did David flee from Nob (*v.10*)? _____________________________________

12. Where did he flee to (*v.10*)? ____

13. Because of his fear of the Philistines, what did David do (*v.13*)?

____

<u>**Applications**</u>:

1. David fled from Saul, and went to Ahimelech, a priest of God. However, when questioned about his mission, David lied to the priest, which later led to the deaths of many. Even if help would have been withheld, David would have been better off telling the truth. Lying always tends to causes future problems, and our God hates it. He wants us to be a truthful people. Do you love the truth, or are you given to lying? Will you determine to work on being an honest person, even to your own hurt? Will you ask God to help you with this?

____

____

2. David lied, because he was afraid. He also pretended to be a madman for the same reason. Fear can cause us to do many things that we should not. Scripture commands us to not be controlled by fear, but the Spirit of God. Are you a fearful person? What are you afraid of right now? Do you believe that God can take care of this for you & give you the strength to confront it? Will you determine to do so?

____

____

____

____

Write down one or more of the above applications that spoke to you personally, and pray that God will help you with it. If you have questions (or need help with application), please speak with your pastor/teacher:

____

____

____

Read I Samuel 22:1-23: Saul Kills the Priests of God

1. Where did David go, to escape from the Philistines (*v.1*)?_____________________________________

2. Who heard about this, and went to David (*v.1*)?

____

3. Who also gathered themselves together with David (*v.2*)?

____

____

4. About how many people were with him (*v.2*)? ____

5. Where did David travel to from the cave (*v.3*)? ______________________________________

6. What did he ask the king to do for him (*v.3-4*)? _____________________________________

7. Who told David to go to Judah (*v.5*)? ____

8. Who heard that David was discovered (*v.6*)?____

9. Who told Saul about David going to Nob (*v.9*)? ______________________________________

10. Who did this man betray to Saul (*v.9-10*)? ____

11. What did Saul accuse the priest of doing (*v.13*)? ___________________________________

12. What was Saul's judgment of Ahimelech (*v.16*)? ____________________________________

13. How many of the priests were slain by Doeg (*v.17-18*)? _____________________________

14. Who escaped from the slaughter (*v.20*)? ____

Applications:

1. David left the Philistines and fled to the cave of Adullam. During this time, his family found out where he was, and went to him, to support him. David's family knew that he had done no wrong, and was following the Lord, so they went to comfort him, in his time of trial. When our family is going through a time of testing, as they follow Christ, we are to offer comfort and aid. Do you love your family and church family this way? When they are hurting, do you pray for and comfort them? If not, will you determine to, in the future? This allows us to prove our Christian love one to another.

____

____

2. After David's family came to him at Adullam, he went to the King of Moab and asked him to take care of his parents. David's great-grandmother, Ruth, was a Moabite, and so the man had family ties with this country, and it was the perfect place for his parents to be out of the reach of Saul's vengeful hand. David understood his responsibility to care for his parents, and honored them this way. Do you love your parents? Do you honor them? When they become older, if they allow you to, will you care for them? What other ways can you show honor to your parents right now?

____

____

____

____

____

Write down one or more of the above applications that spoke to you personally, and pray that God will help you with it. If you have questions (or need help with application), please speak with your pastor/teacher:

____

____

____

<u>**Read I Samuel 23:1-29: David Flees to Ziph**</u>

1. Who were the Philistines fighting against (*v.1*)? ____

2. Who told David to go and save these people (*v.2*)?____

3. What was the mental state of David's men (*v.3*)? ____

4. What did God promise David (*v.4*)?

____

5. What did Abiathar bring with him, when he fled to David (*v.6*)?_________________________________

6. Who found out that David was in Keilah (*v.7*)? ____

7. What did God tell David that the men of Keilah would do to him (*v.12*)?

____

8. About how many men did David have with him (*v.13*)? _________________________________

9. Did David and his men escape from Keilah (*v.13*)?____

10. Where did David go to hide from Saul (*v.14*)? ____

11. Who went to strengthen David's hand at this place (*v.16*)? _________________________________

12. What did Jonathan declare about David (*v.17*)? ____

13. Who told Saul where David was (*v.19*)?____

14. What caused Saul to return from pursuing after David (*v.27-28*)?

____

15. Where did David end up staying (*v.29*)?____

<u>**Applications**</u>:

1. David heard about the Philistines raiding Keilah, and God gave him leave to go into battle.
Nonetheless, David's men were afraid, so he inquired of the Lord again, to confirm God's will. We do not
rely on ephods for prayer, but can pray at any time. We also have God's Word to confirm His will for us.
Do you read God's Word every day? Do you rely on its commands and principles to guard and guide your
life? Will you trust it above the fickle opinions of human beings and your emotions?

____

____

2. Sadly, the people of Keilah betrayed David to Saul, but God gave him forewarning of it. When people are following Christ, we ought to be loyal to them (instead of betraying them). However, when we fear people, we will bend and sway with the wind: going whichever way is easiest. Are you a person that stands by God's people and His Word, or do you follow the easiest crowd and standards? When was a time that you stood for God's Word, or His people, when it was not easy to do so?

____

____

____

____

3. David was a man on the run from Saul, but Saul was a man on the run from God. The king had traveled so far down the path of sin that he was deluded into thinking that he was the victim! Sin causes insanity. It draws us far from the side of God, and causes us to have delusions about our state in life. Saul was not a victim, but an offender! He was not right with God, but put on a pretense of it. How is your walk with Christ right now? Are you moving farther away from Him, or closer to Him? Are you living a life more in the flesh, or in the Spirit? How do you know this?

____

____

____

____

Write down one or more of the above applications that spoke to you personally, and pray that God will help you with it. If you have questions (or need help with application), please speak with your pastor/teacher:

____

____

____

<u>Read I Samuel 24:1-22: David Spares Saul's Life</u>

1. Where did Saul learn that David was hiding (**v.1**)?_________________________________

2. How many chosen men did Saul take with him (**v.2**)? _________________________________

3. While Saul was occupied in the cave, what did David do to him (**v.4**)?

____

4. Why did David feel guilty about doing this to Saul (**v.6**)?

____

5. After David cried out to Saul, what did he do (**v.8**)?

____

6. What did David state to Saul about their situation (**v.12**)?

____

____

7. What proverb of the ancients did David quote (**v.13**)?

____

8. How did Saul respond to David's words (**v.16**)?

____

9. What did he admit to David (**v.17**)?

____

10. What did Saul declare to David (**v.20**)?

____

11. Where did Saul go, after this confrontation (**v.22**)? _________________________________

12. Where did David go (**v.22**)? _________________________________

<u>**Applications**</u>:

1. David was a man of integrity and faith. He was afraid, but refused to raise a hand against Saul. In fact, he was so sensitive to this that, when he cut the skirt from Saul's robe, he was convicted by it. David believed that God would deal with Saul. God put Saul on the throne, and He would take him off, when the time was right. Do you have faith like that? Do you trust God to take care of your needs? Do you pray and trust that He will work in your life & the lives of others, or do you have to be in control of every situation? When was a time that you took your hands off the steering wheel of your life, and allowed God to take control?

____

____

____

____

2. Not only was David a man of integrity, but he was not foolish. He knew the path that Saul was traveling. He knew that his sin caused him to have fickle judgment. So, when Saul promised to leave David alone, David did not go back to Jerusalem, but stayed in the wilderness. Faith trusts in God, but wisdom grants common sense. We need to learn the balance between faith and foolishness. Thankfully, the Bible promotes such a balance. Do you prove all things, or just believe whatever people tell you? Is your standard for such proving the Bible, or something/someone else? Do you work at finding the balance between faith and foolishness?

____

____

____

Write down one or more of the above applications that spoke to you personally, and pray that God will help you with it. If you have questions (or need help with application), please speak with your pastor/teacher:

____

____

____

<u>Read I Samuel 25:1-17: David and Nabal</u>

1. What prophet of God died (*v.1*)? _______________________________________

2. Where was he buried (*v.1*)? _______________________________________

3. What was the name of Nabal's wife (*v.3*)? _______________________________________

4. What was special about her (*v.3*)?

____

5. How does the Bible describe Nabal (*v.3*)?

____

6. What was Nabal doing in the wilderness (*v.4*)? _______________________________________

7. Who did David send to Nabal (*v.5*)? _______________________________________

8. Because David helped Nabal's sheep, what did he ask of him (*v.8*)?

____

9. Did Nabal help David (*v.10-12*)? _______________________________________

10. What was David's response (*v.13*)?

____

11. Who was told about Nabal's treatment of David's men (*v.14*)? _______________________________________

12. Why could no one reason with Nabal (*v.17*)?

____

<u>**Applications**</u>:

1. Nabal was a wicked man that lived a foolish life, but had many goods in this world. We live in a day in which many believers think that, if we follow Christ, He will make us rich and powerful. This is simply not true! In fact, many godly believers are also the most poor, by this world's standards. Nabal is the perfect example a wicked man that had many goods. The key for the believer is not to love money, but to be content with what God gives us. Do you want to be rich in this world's goods, or in heavenly treasure? Do you love money, or are you satisfied with what God provides for you?

____

____

2. Abigail was a wise woman that married a wicked man. No doubt, her husband's ungodliness grieved her heart daily. This is a challenge to every believer to ensure that we marry fellow believers in Jesus Christ. In addition, we ought to marry believers that will help us to become better for Christ. If you are unmarried, will you determine to marry a believer that will help your walk with Christ? If you are married, will you determine to be a believer that will be a good testimony before your spouse, like Abigail was?

____

____

____

Write down one or more of the above applications that spoke to you personally, and pray that God will help you with it. If you have questions (or need help with application), please speak with your pastor/teacher:

____

____

____

1. Because of Nabal's actions, how did Abigail respond (*v.18*)?

____

____

2. Did she tell Nabal (*v.19*)? ____

3. What did David say that Nabal had done to him (*v.21*)?

____

4. How did Abigail come before David (*v.23*)? ________________________________

5. What sort of battles did Abigail say that David fought (*v.28*)?_________________________

6. What did she say that God would appoint him as (*v.30*)? _________________________

7. What did David say that Abigail had caused him to avoid (*v.33*)?

____

8. How did he tell her to return to her house (*v.35*)?________________________________

9. What was Nabal holding in his house, when Abigail arrived (*v.36*)? ______________________

10. What happened to Nabal, when his wife told him about what she did for David (*v.37*)?

____

11. Why did Nabal die (*v.38*)?____

12. After Nabal's death, who became David's wife (*v.39-42*)?______________________________

Applications:

1. Nabal was a foolish man, but he had a wise wife. Abigal sought to make peace with David by admitting Nabal's fault, and giving him a gift for his men. Jesus tells us that we are blessed, if we seek to make peace with others. In doing so, we prove that we are God's children. Are you a person that seeks to make peace, or one that enjoys conflict? Are you willing to walk away from a bad situation, in the effort of keeping the peace? When was a time that you have done this?

____

____

____

2. David wisely ceased from seeking to avenge himself, and allowed himself to be sated by Abigal. Later on, we see God avenging David in the form of causing Nabal to be smitten with a health problem and die. The Bible teaches us to trust in God for justice. It teaches that revenge belongs to God. He is the perfect judge, jury, and executioner. Are you willing to forgive, instead of seeking revenge against others that do you wrong? Are you willing to commend justice and judgment to God, instead of seeking vengeance for yourself? Name a time where you forgave someone, instead of seeking revenge on them:

____

____

____

____

Write down one or more of the above applications that spoke to you personally, and pray that God will help you with it. If you have questions (or need help with application), please speak with your pastor/teacher:

____

____

____

<u>Read I Samuel 26:1-25: David Spares Saul's Life (Again)</u>

1. Who told Saul where David was hiding (*v.1*)? _______________________________

2. Where was David hiding (*v.1*)? _______________________________

3. How many chosen men did Saul bring with him (*v.3*)? _______________________________

4. What did David send out, to scout Saul's party (*v.4*)? _______________________________

5. Who went down with David into Saul's camp (*v.6*)? _______________________________

6. What did this man want to do to Saul (*v.8*)? _______________________________

7. What did David say would happen to Saul (*v.10*)?

____

____

8. What did he refuse to do to Saul (*v.11*)? _______________________________

9. What did they take from the camp instead (*v.11*)? _______________________________

10. Why did no one see David do these things (*v.12*)?

____

11. Who was supposed to guard the king's life (*v.13-15*)?_______________________________

12. What did David say that this man was worthy of (*v.16*)?_______________________________

13. After David defended his innocence before Saul, what did the king say (*v.21*)?

____

____

<u>**Applications**</u>:

1. Once more, God allows Saul to fall into David's hand and, again, David commends the king's fate to God. In fact, David was tempted by Abishai to slay the king, and he would not. In reference to the previous chapter, David shows his faith that God would deal with Saul. People will cause us trouble, and, if we choose to live for Christ, it is guaranteed. But, we are commanded to trust in God's ability to take care of us. Do you believe that God is better at giving out justice than you? Do you believe that He will take care of you, if you follow Him? When have you seen Him do this for you?

____

____

____

2. As David addressed Saul, he referred to himself as a flea. In other words, he felt himself insignificant, and beneath the notice of the king. Here we see David's humility. Not only would he not lift a hand against God's chosen king, but did not think himself worth pursuing. Humility is required of a person to both trust in Christ for salvation, and follow Him as His disciple. Have you done this? Have you humbled yourself to receive God's salvation by faith in Jesus Christ? Do you work to be humble: following Christ in His Word day by day?

____

____

____

Write down one or more of the above applications that spoke to you personally, and pray that God will help you with it. If you have questions (or need help with application), please speak with your pastor/teacher:

____

____

____

<u>**Read I Samuel 27:1-12: David Flees Back to the Philistines**</u>

1. After the previous incident with Saul, what did David say in his heart (***v.1***)?

____

2. Where did he determine to escape to (***v.1***)? ____

3. How many men were with David (***v.2***)? ____

4. Which king did he flee to (***v.2***)? ____

5. What happened, when Saul heard about this (***v.4***)?

____

6. What city did Achish give to David, to dwell in (***v.6***)?_______________________________

7. How long did David dwell with the Philistines (***v.7***)? ________________________________

8. Who did David choose to invade and destroy (***v.8***)?

____

9. Where did he tell Achish that he was invading and destroying (***v.10***)?

____

10. Did Achish believe David's lies (***v.12***)? ____

11. What did he say to himself about David (***v.12***)?

____

<u>**Applications**</u>:

1. Previously, we saw David's faith and humility. However, at some point soon after the most recent incident with Saul, the man lost faith and decided that he was going to die at the hand of the king. This was pure assumption and faithlessness. God had told David that he would be king, and had not changed His mind. Nonetheless, we see dangerous assumptions being made here. When we assume, we often get into trouble. God has given us His Word, so that we can believe and be guided by it. He does not want us to live by fear, worry, or assumption. When was a time that you assumed and regretted it?

____

____

____

2. In relation to the previous question, are you a person that is prone to fear, worry, and assumption? Do you work at trusting wholly in God's Word, instead of your own thoughts? When was a time when you trusted in God's Word, and saw God prove Himself to you, because you did?

____

____

____

____

3. David was a man of faith and fearlessness one minute, and faithlessness and fear the next. This ought to warn us that, if a faithful man like David can fall into fear and assumption, then so can we. Thus, we need to learn to guard our lives, and be spiritually renewed daily. This only happens through a thriving devotional life. Do you guard your devotional life? When do you read your Bible and pray every day? Do you make sure to be in church whenever possible?

____

____

____

Write down one or more of the above applications that spoke to you personally, and pray that God will help you with it. If you have questions (or need help with application), please speak with your pastor/teacher:

____

____

____

Read I Samuel 28:1-25: Saul and the Witch of Endor

1. Who gathered their armies together, to fight with Israel (*v.1*)? _______________________________

2. Who wanted David to go with him into battle (*v.1*)? _______________________________________

3. Who was dead, at this time (*v.3*)? ____

4. What had Saul put out of the land (*v.3*)?

____

5. When Saul saw the Philistine army, how did he react (*v.5*)?

____

6. What happened, when he went to inquire of the Lord through various means (*v.6*)?

____

7. Because of this, what did Saul command his servants to seek out (*v.7*)?

____

8. Where did they find one (*v.7*)? ____

9. Did the woman initially want to help Saul (*v.9*)? _______________________________

10. Whose spirit did Saul ask the woman to bring up (*v.11*)? ___________________________

11. Why did Samuel's spirit say that God was not answering Saul (*v.16*)?

____

12. Who did God purpose to give the kingdom to (*v.17*)? _______________________________

13. Where did Samuel say that Saul and his sons would be, by the next day (*v.19*)?

____

14. How did Saul respond to this (*v.20*)?

____

<u>**Applications**</u>:

1. Saul was afraid of the coming battle with the Philistines. He did the right thing and prayed to God for guidance and help. However, God did not answer, because Saul was not right with Him. A long time ago, the king determined to be filled with pride, and thus his relationship with the God of Heaven was stymied. God resists the proud, but gives grace to the humble. If we want God to speak to us in His Word, answer our prayers, and use us for His glory, then we need to humble ourselves before Him. Do you work to be humble? Have you surrendered your life to God? Have you surrendered your will, plans, and desires? There is no greater, more exciting life than the one surrendered to Christ.

____

2. Because Saul did not receive an answer to his prayers, he went further outside of God's will, to seek the desired information. God's silence was meant to force the self-examination of Saul's heart, with the desired end result being repentance and restoration. Instead, the prideful king thought that God needed to work on his timetable. Pride makes us to lose patience, but humility waits on the Lord. Some of the worst decisions are made in a rush. Are you a person that waits for God to answer, or one that loses patience with Him quickly? When was a time that you were patient with God, and He answered your prayers? Did it encourage you to be patient in the future?

____

____

____

3. In reference to the previous question, we understand that Saul was not patient or humble before God. As such, he went outside of God's Law, to calm his troubled soul, and thought that such peace would be found by inquiring of a witch, who raised the spirit of Samuel. The experience only served to trouble Saul further. Going outside of God's will always causes more trouble than peace. True peace only comes by trusting in God's Word. Have you found this to be true? When was a time that you trusted in God's promises, and received great peace?

____

____

____

Write down one or more of the above applications that spoke to you personally, and pray that God will help you with it. If you have questions (or need help with application), please speak with your pastor/teacher:

____

____

<u>Read I Samuel 29:1-11: David Is Rejected by the Philistines</u>

1. Where did the Philistines gather their armies together (**v.1**)?________________________

2. Where did the Israelites pitch by (**v.1**)? ____

3. Who passed on in the rereward with Achish (**v.2**)? _________________________________

4. How did the princes of the Philistines respond to this man's presence (**v.4**)?

____

5. What did they want Achish to do with him (**v.4**)?

____

6. What song had been sung about David (**v.5**)?

____

7. What had Achish not found in David, since the day of his coming to him (**v.6**)?___________

8. Why did he want him to return and go in peace (**v.7**)?

____

9. What was David like to Achish (**v.9**)? ____

10. Where did David and his men depart into (**v.11**)? ________________________________

11. Where did the Philistines go to (**v.11**)?____

<u>Applications</u>:

1. King Achish came to foolishly trust David. David put on a guise of aligning himself with the Philistines, but actually fought against the enemies of Israel (instead of the Jews themselves). Achish came to believe David's lies, and went so far as to place the man and his troops in the rereward of the Philistine army. The rereward was the troop that protected the back ranks of the army. It was a strategically important position. Achish's foolishness teaches us to be careful who we trust. God commands us to prove all things: being a discerning people. Who do you trust? How far do you trust them? Why? What have they done to be worthy of your trust? Are they godly individuals? Who are they?

____

____

____

2. The other kings of the Philistines were naturally suspicious of David's presence in the Philistine army. Here was a man known for killing Philistines, and had been a powerful enemy! Of course they would be suspicious, no matter the story that David told! In light of this, and the previous question, do you seek to be a discerning person? Do you work to prove all things, instead of just believing whatever people tell you? Do you measure what you see and hear against the principles given in God's Word? How have you been proven to have good discernment recently?

____

____

____

Write down one or more of the above applications that spoke to you personally, and pray that God will help you with it. If you have questions (or need help with application), please speak with your pastor/teacher:

____

____

____

Read I Samuel 30:1-10: David Returns to Ziklag

1. What group of people had invaded the south (*v.1*)? _______________________________________

2. What had they done to Ziklag (*v.1*)?_______________________________________

3. What did they do with the inhabitants of Ziklag (*v.2*)?

____

4. When David and his men came to Ziklag, and saw it burned, how did they respond (*v.4*)?

____

5. What did the men talk about doing to David (*v.6*)? _______________________________________

6. Why (*v.6*)?_______________________________________

7. How did David encourage himself (*v.6*)? _______________________________________

8. What did he have Abiathar bring to him (*v.7*)? _______________________________________

9. After praying to God for direction, what did He say (*v.8*)?

____

10. How many men were with David (*v.9*)? _______________________________________

11. How many men stayed behind with the stuff (*v.10*)? _______________________________________

12. Why (*v.10*)?_______________________________________

Applications:

1. David had lost hope. He believed that Saul would kill him one day, so he left to be among the Philistines. Despite the perceived circumstances, God had not changed his mind about making David to be king. If David would have asked God, he surely would have found this truth out. Just because our circumstances change does not mean that God has changed His mind, promises, or Word. Usually, our circumstances change, because God is testing our faith. Have you ever seen this in your life? How did you respond? Did your faith grow, because God proved Himself to you?

____

____

____

____

2. In reference to the previous question, we find David losing hope and making decisions without God's input. Because of this, God had to get David's attention. Allowing the Amalekites to burn Ziklag had the desired effect. At times, we get away from God. In response, He reaches out, to bring us back to Him. The Bible calls this chastisement. The purpose of chastisement is to make our lives uncomfortable, so that we will follow Christ anew. Have you ever seen God's chastening hand in your life? In what way? How did you respond?

____

____

____

____

3. When God got David's attention, he did two things: remembered God's Word and prayed. The Bible says that David encouraged himself in the Lord. This is only possible by considering the Word of God. Furthermore, he sought God's orders on how to deal with the situation at Ziklag. Because David did these two things, he received his family back alive. Bible reading and prayer are essential to our spiritual health. They teach us who God is, as well as His will for our lives. Do you read your Bible and pray regularly? Can you see your spiritual walk getting stronger, as you do? In what way?

____

____

____

____

Write down one or more of the above applications that spoke to you personally, and pray that God will help you with it. If you have questions (or need help with application), please speak with your pastor/teacher:

____

____

____

<u>Read I Samuel 30:11-31: David Returns to Ziklag (Part Two)</u>

1. Who did David and his men find in a field (***v.11***)? _________________________________

2. How did they treat this man (***v.11-12***)?

____

3. Why was the servant left behind (***v.13***)? _____________________________________

4. What did this man make David swear to him, in exchange for leading them to the Amalekites (***v.15***)?

____

5. What were the Amalekites doing, when David found them (***v.16***)?

____

6. For how long did David fight against the Amalekites (***v.17***)?

____

7. How much of what was lost did David and his men recover (***v.18***)? _______________________

8. What did the wicked men in David's army want to do with those that had to stay behind (***v.22***)?

____

9. Did David agree to this (***v.23***)? ____

10. What did David make in regards to that matter from that day forward (***v.25***)?

____

11. Who did David send part of the spoil to (***v.26***)?_______________________________

<u>Applications</u>:

1. David and his men found an Egyptian servant to the Amalekites, as they sought for their families. In their very emotional state, they could have taken their anger and grief out on the man, but did not. Instead, they showed him kindness, and he showed them where the Amalekites were. No matter our emotional state, God can help us to control ourselves. This is called temperance. How are you at controlling your emotions? Are you very emotional? Do you act inappropriately, at times? Will you ask God to help you to always act in a way that pleases Him?

____

____

2. David and his men were very tired. In fact, part of his troops had to stay behind, because of their weary state. Nonetheless, the small army was given the strength to seek the Amalekites and fight for another whole day, because of their faith! God is able to help us, when we follow Him. He is able to give us strength, skill, knowledge, and whatever else we need, to get the job done. Has God ever done this for you? What was the situation? How did God provide perfectly for you? What did it do for your faith?

____

____

____

____

3. God had promised David that he would recover everything, if he pursued after the Amalekites. David was not promised that he would recover fifty percent, twenty-five, or ninety-nine. It was promised that he would recover everything, and he did. God keeps His promises. When He says, "All," He means, "All." Have you ever seen God specifically meet your needs in such a way? What was the situation? Did it build your faith? Did you give God the glory?

____

____

____

____

Write down one or more of the above applications that spoke to you personally, and pray that God will help you with it. If you have questions (or need help with application), please speak with your pastor/teacher:

____

____

____

Read I Samuel 31:1-13: Saul Is Defeated and Killed

1. Who fought against Israel (*v.1*)?____

2. Who fell down slain in Mount Gilboa (*v.1*)? ___________________________________

3. Who did the Philistines follow hard upon (*v.2*)? ______________________________

4. Who did they slay (*v.2*)? ____

5. What happened to Saul (*v.3*)? ____

6. What did he want his armor-bearer to do to him (*v.4*)? _______________________

7. Did the man obey (*v.4*)? ____

8. What did Saul do, in response (*v.4*)? ____

9. What did the armor-bearer do, when he saw this (*v.5*)?

____

10. What did the Philistines do, when they found Saul (*v.9*)?

____

11. Where did they put his armor (*v.10*)? _______________________________________

12. Who heard of what had happened to Saul (*v.11*)?_____________________________

13. What did the valiant men of this city do (*v.12-13*)?

____

____

Applications:

1. Saul's sin finally caught up to him (as they say). He was certain that he and his sons would be on the throne of Israel for many years (despite the promise of God). But, in the end, God proved Himself yet again. God is sovereign. He is the God of the Universe with a great plan for it. The best thing for us to do is believe in and follow him. Saul neglected to do that, and greatly suffered for it. Do you believe that God is sovereign? Have you trusted in Jesus Christ as your Savior? How have you worked to follow Christ, since you trusted in Him?

____

____

2. Saul refused God's design for the Kingdom of Israel. He had been refused as king, and David was to reign in his place. When Samuel told the man these words, Saul should have stepped down from the throne immediately. Instead, he stubbornly rejected God's will. This caused many people in Saul's family and the entire nation to suffer. One man's pride caused the pain of many. We need to be careful to humble ourselves, and do God's will for our lives. If we do, then God will truly bless us. If we do not, then God will truly chastise us. These often extend to our loved ones in ways that we cannot imagine. Are you determined to follow Christ, or are you determined to follow your own flesh? Have you seen God bless or curse others, because they chose to follow or ignore Him? How have you seen this?

____

____

____

____

Write down one or more of the above applications that spoke to you personally, and pray that God will help you with it. If you have questions (or need help with application), please speak with your pastor/teacher:

____

____

____